THE
WALES
QUIZ BOOK

Thanks to my editor, Carolyn Hodges

THE WALES QUIZ BOOK

FIENDISH QUIZZES ABOUT ALL THINGS WELSH!

MATTHEW JONES

First impression: 2018

© Matthew Jones and Y Lolfa Cyf., 2018

Cover design: Y Lolfa

ISBN: 978 1 78461 521 5

Published and printed in Wales
on paper from well maintained forests by
Y Lolfa Cyf., Talybont, Ceredigion SY24 5HE
website www.ylolfa.com
e-mail ylolfa@ylolfa.com
tel 01970 832 304
fax 832 782

Introduction

It's always fun to test your own knowledge, and even better to challenge others. Here's your chance to prove to yourself or to your family and friends how much you know about Wales. You don't need a degree in Welsh history (although I'm sure it couldn't harm!) to enjoy this book, as it's a mixture of music, films, successful individuals, memorable events, geography and much more.

Some questions are harder than others, but there are plenty of multiple-choice options, which means everyone has a fighting chance of getting some right. Good luck!

Matthew Jones
February 2018

Questions

Round 1

1. **In which of the following towns was the Grand Pavilion opened in 1932?**
   a) Porthcawl
   b) Tenby
   c) Aberaeron

2. **When did the national census first ask the inhabitants of Wales if they could speak Welsh?**
   a) 1851
   b) 1871
   c) 1891

3. **Which BBC television programme has been presented by Tim Vincent and Gethin Jones?**
   a) *Top of the Pops*
   b) *Blue Peter*
   c) *Live & Kicking*

4. **Mary Hopkin achieved a UK number one single in 1968 while signed to the Beatles-founded Apple Records label. What was the song?**
   a) 'Goodbye'
   b) 'Let My Name Be Sorrow'
   c) 'Those Were the Days'

5. **Which town is situated at the site of a previous Roman fort known as Burrium?**

     a) Montgomery
     b) Monmouth
     c) Usk

6. **Which character did Haverfordwest-born Rhys Ifans play in the 1999 Richard Curtis-written film *Notting Hill*?**

     a) William Thacker
     b) Spike
     c) Rufus the Thief

7. **Which small mining village was struck by tragedy when 144 people, including 116 children, were tragically killed in 1966 after a coal tip slid down a mountain engulfing several houses and Pantglas Junior School?**

     a) Troedyrhiw
     b) Beaufort
     c) Aberfan

8. **The 1982 film *Firefox* was produced by, directed by and starred Clint Eastwood. The film is based on the novel of the same name by which author?**

9. **On 13 May 1897, Italian inventor Guglielmo Marconi assisted by George Kemp, a Cardiff-based post office engineer, transmitted the first wireless signal over open sea. The signal was sent between Lavernock Point near Penarth and which island?**

10. **Richard Lewis was hanged at Cardiff Gaol in 1831 for stabbing soldier Donald Black in the leg during riots on the streets of Merthyr. Years later, Ianto Parker confessed to the crime on his deathbed. By what name was Richard Lewis better known?**

Round 2

1. **Which is the longest river in Britain, flowing from the Cambrian Mountains to the Bristol Channel?**
   - a) Dee
   - b) Severn
   - c) Teifi

2. **Which mountain, 886 metres in height, is the tallest in Wales outside Snowdonia?**
   - a) Cribyn
   - b) Fan Brycheiniog
   - c) Pen y Fan

3. **Ferndale-born Stanley Baker produced and starred in the 1964 film *Zulu*. Which battle does the film depict?**
   - a) Battle of Kambula
   - b) Siege of Eshowe
   - c) Battle of Rorke's Drift

4. **Mary Quant was an influential figure in British fashion during the 1960s. In 1955, her first boutique was opened on the King's Road in London. What was it called?**
   - a) Mod
   - b) Bazaar
   - c) Quant by Quant

5. **Who did John Cale collaborate with to produce the 1990-released album *Songs for Drella*?**
   - a) Lou Reed
   - b) David Bowie
   - c) Bob Dylan

6. **In 1904, brothers Walter and Tom Davies from Llanelli invented the first motor car spare wheel. What was it called?**

    a) The Stradey Spare Wheel
    b) The Stepney Spare Motor Wheel
    c) The Davies Circle

7. **In rugby league, Billy Boston scored 478 tries in 487 matches for Wigan. For which rugby union club did he make a single appearance on 26 December 1952?**

    a) Pontypridd
    b) Glamorgan Wanderers
    c) Cardiff

8. **Who in December 1910 became the first person to make an airship crossing of the English Channel at night?**

9. **In which 1968 film starring Jane Fonda was 'Llanfairpwllgwyngyllgogerychwyrndrobwllllantysiliogogogoch' used as the password for the headquarters of the resistance leader?**

10. **The Menai Suspension Bridge was opened on 30 January 1826, making it the longest suspension bridge in the world at the time. Which Scottish engineer was the bridge's designer?**

Round 3

1. **Who is the patron saint of Wales?**

    a) St David
    b) St George
    c) St Patrick

2. **Anthony Hopkins earned a Best Actor Academy Award for his portrayal of Hannibal Lecter in a 1991-released film. What was the film called?**

    a) *Manhunter*
    b) *The Silence of the Lambs*
    c) *Red Dragon*

3. **In which year did the number of passengers using Cardiff Airport pass one million for the first time?**

    a) 1986
    b) 1994
    c) 2001

4. **In which town was Owain Glyndŵr crowned Prince of Wales in 1404?**

    a) Machynlleth
    b) Caernarfon
    c) Aberystwyth

5. **The Alarm played their first gig at Prestatyn's Royal Victoria public house in 1981. In 2004, they duped the music industry by releasing their single '45 RPM' under a pseudonym. What was this alternative group name?**

    a) Lipsynch
    b) Teenage Drama Queens
    c) The Poppy Fields

6. **The Point of Ayr lighthouse was built in 1777. What was the annual salary of Edward Price, its first lighthouse keeper?**

   a) eight guineas

   b) twelve guineas

   c) sixteen guineas

7. **In 1973, the Wales rugby union side defeated Australia 24-0 at Cardiff Arms Park. Allan Martin and Clive Shell made their international debuts in the game. Which club did they both play for?**

   a) Aberavon

   b) London Welsh

   c) Bridgend

8. **Where in north Wales did Butlins open a holiday camp in 1947?**

9. **Lord Ninian Edward Crichton-Stuart was shot in the head while serving with the 6th Battalion Welsh Regiment on 2 October 1915. He was Wales' only Member of Parliament to be killed in the first World War. Which party did he represent at Westminster?**

10. **Pryce Pryce-Jones started his working life at the age of twelve as an apprentice at a drapery firm. Which type of business is he credited with inventing?**

Round 4

1. **In which valley will you find the towns of Aberdare and Mountain Ash?**
   a) Cynon
   b) Rhymney
   c) Sirhowy

2. **Argyll Gardens, Cockett Woods and Singleton Park can be found in which city?**
   a) Bangor
   b) St Asaph
   c) Swansea

3. **Who became the first Welsh singer to gain a UK number one single, with the song 'As I Love You' in January 1959?**
   a) Shirley Bassey
   b) Iris Williams
   c) Dorothy Squires

4. **Scottish socialist Keir Hardie made history by becoming the first Labour Party Member of Parliament. Which constituency did he represent from 1900 until 1915?**
   a) Rhondda
   b) Merthyr Tydfil
   c) East Glamorganshire

5. **Which castle was the scene of the surrender of Richard II to Henry Bolingbroke in 1399?**

   a) Flint
   b) Ewloe
   c) Hawarden

6. **Which city hosted the modern National Eisteddfod for a third time in 1929?**

   a) Bristol
   b) London
   c) Liverpool

7. **Edgar Evans was born on 7 March 1876 near Rhossili on the Gower Peninsula. What did he achieve prior to his death on 17 February 1912?**

   a) first person to fly from Europe to Africa
   b) first Welshman to reach the South Pole
   c) first European to sail across the Atlantic single-handed

8. **Who in 1972 became the oldest person to be knighted when he received the honour at the age of 88, for services to the preservation of the environment and to architecture?**

9. **Who left the British government with a resignation speech at Westminster on 13 November 1990 attacking Prime Minister Margaret Thatcher, comparing her treatment of her subordinates negotiating in Europe to a cricket captain sending his opening batsmen to the crease, having first broken their bats?**

10. *Mochyn* is the Welsh word for which animal?

Round 5

1. **In which year did Wales ban smoking in enclosed public spaces?**

   a) 2003

   b) 2005

   c) 2007

2. **Where was the UK's first open-air museum opened in 1948?**

   a) St Fagans

   b) Llangollen

   c) Tredegar

3. **Which river was dammed in the 1970s to form the Llyn Brianne reservoir?**

   a) Teifi

   b) Gwili

   c) Towy

4. **In which 1966 black comedy-drama did Richard Burton play George opposite Elizabeth Taylor's Martha, a role for which he was nominated for a Best Actor Academy Award?**

   a) *The Taming of the Shrew*

   b) *Who's Afraid of Virginia Woolf?*

   c) *The Spy Who Came in from the Cold*

5. **Second World War fighter pilot Robert Everett was buried at Llanddona, Anglesey after his Hurricane plane crashed there in January 1942. What did he achieve in 1929?**

a) invented the electric razor

b) won the Grand National on the horse Gregalach at odds of 100-1

c) became Australia's youngest Prime Minister

6. **While campaigning for the 1802 General Election, William Paxton pledged to build a bridge across the river Towy. He failed to win the Carmarthen seat and instead spent the money on Paxton Tower. How much money did he spend on erecting it?**

a) £2,000

b) £8,000

c) £15,000

7. **Alex Jones became the presenter of which BBC programme in 2010?**

a) *Homes Under the Hammer*

b) *Strictly Come Dancing*

c) *The One Show*

8. **In which town was a bronze statue of comedian Tommy Cooper, created by James Done, unveiled in 2008?**

9. **What was the name of the single-hull oil tanker that hit rocks when entering the Cleddau Estuary on 15 February 1996, spilling 72,000 tonnes of crude oil into the sea?**

10. **Thomas Jones was born in 1530, becoming an outlaw by the age of eighteen with a Robin Hood style of crusade to redistribute wealth. What was he better known as?**

Round 6

1. **In which city was the Wales Millennium Centre opened in 2004?**

    a) Newport

    b) Swansea

    c) Cardiff

2. **Which father and son pairing were inducted together into the Welsh Sports Hall of Fame in 2015?**

    a) Derek and Scott Quinnell (rugby union)

    b) Jeff and Simon Jones (cricket)

    c) Mel and Jeremy Charles (football)

3. **In which of the following counties would you find the towns of Cardigan, Aberystwyth and Tregaron?**

    a) Ceredigion

    b) Pembrokeshire

    c) Powys

4. **Glyn Wise, Imogen Thomas and Helen Adams were all contestants on which reality television programme?**

    a) *The X Factor*

    b) *Big Brother*

    c) *Britain's Got Talent*

5. **In which year was the first Severn Bridge opened, replacing a vehicle ferry service between Aust Cliff and Beachley Peninsula?**

    a) 1959

    b) 1966

    c) 1974

6. **Which comedian said 'In the Bible, God made it rain for 40 days and 40 nights. That's a pretty good summer for Wales. That's a hosepipe ban waiting to happen.'?**

   a) Paul Whitehouse

   b) Rhod Gilbert

   c) Lloyd Langford

7. **Which role did Ioan Gruffudd play in the 2005 film *Fantastic Four*?**

   a) Reed Richards

   b) Johnny Storm

   c) Ben Grimm

8. **Who became the first British President of the European Commission in 1977?**

9. **The Brunt Ice Shelf in Antarctica was named after which meteorologist, who received a knighthood in 1949 and was appointed Knight Commander of the order of the British Empire in 1959?**

10. **Launched in 1804, what was the first weekly newspaper published in Wales?**

Round 7

1. **_Melyn_ is the Welsh word for which colour?**
   - a) red
   - b) blue
   - c) yellow

2. **Where in Wales would you find the mountain Cadair Idris?**
   - a) Gwynedd
   - b) Powys
   - c) Monmouthshire

3. **On which island did St Cadfan establish a monastic settlement in the sixth century?**
   - a) Skomer Island
   - b) Bardsey Island
   - c) Caldey Island

4. **In which city was the National Waterfront Museum opened in 2005?**
   - a) Newport
   - b) Cardiff
   - c) Swansea

5. **Who, during his tenure as Secretary of State for Wales from 1993 until 1995, was infamously caught on television cameras unable to sing the Welsh national anthem, embarrassingly mouthing the words incorrectly?**
   - a) Peter Walker
   - b) John Redwood
   - c) William Hague

6. **Which role did Swansea-born Talfryn Thomas play in the BBC comedy series *Dad's Army* during the 1970s?**

   a) Mr/Private Cheeseman
   b) Warden Hodges
   c) Captain Square

7. **Serious civil unrest broke out in the countryside of south-west Wales in 1839, which continued until 1843. This was due to several factors, including the punitive effect of toll gates. What was the action known as?**

   a) Sons of Llywelyn Uproar
   b) The Rebecca Riots
   c) Glyndwr's Upheaval

8. **In which town was the Pontlottyn department store established in the 1870s, closing its doors for the last time in the 1960s?**

9. **William Jones published his seminal work *Synopsis Palmariorum Matheseos* in 1706, where he introduced a symbol for the constant ratio of the circumference to diameter of a circle. What was this symbol?**

10. **The first season of *The X Factor* in the United States of America was aired in 2011. Who was the show's first presenter?**

Round 8

1. **Rhythm guitarist and lyricist Richey Edwards went missing in February 1995, with his car being found by the Severn Bridge. Which band was he a member of?**

    a) Manic Street Preachers
    b) Melys
    c) The Crocketts

2. **What was the population of Wales when the first official census was undertaken in 1801?**

    a) 463,000
    b) 511,000
    c) 587,000

3. **Which road runs from Llandudno in north Wales to Cardiff in the south?**

    a) A44
    b) A470
    c) M48

4. **Where in 1067 did the construction of the first castle in Wales begin?**

    a) Caergwrle
    b) Dinas Bran
    c) Chepstow

5. **In which ITV comedy series did Windsor Davies play the character Oliver Smallbridge opposite Donald Sinden's character Simon Peel?**

    a) *Ever Decreasing Circles*
    b) *Only When I Laugh*
    c) *Never the Twain*

6. **Who was named BBC Sports Personality of the Year in 2009?**

   a) Shane Williams
   b) Ryan Giggs
   c) Joe Calzaghe

7. **In 1928 Amelia Earhart became the first woman to fly across the Atlantic Ocean. The plane left Trepassy, Newfoundland on Sunday 17 June, landing in Wales at approximately 12:40pm on the following day. In which harbour did the plane land?**

   a) Burry Port
   b) Milford Haven
   c) Pwllheli

8. **Which fruit has a variety called Lloyd George, having been named after the former British Prime Minister?**

9. **In which Cardiff-based, 1959 film did John Mills play a detective seeking to prise incriminating details from a young girl played by his real-life daughter Hayley?**

10. **In rugby union, Wales defeated England 24-15 in 1985. Which Neath player made a try-scoring debut in the match?**

Round 9

1. **What was the name of the village drowned in 1965 to form the Llyn Celyn reservoir to provide water for the city of Liverpool?**

   a) Eglwys Celyn

   b) Capel Celyn

   c) Celyn Ffestiniog

2. **Which mansion inspired the setting for Beatrix Potter's book *The Tale of the Flopsy Bunnies*?**

   a) Glanbrydan Park, Llandeilo

   b) Trevalyn Manor, Rossett

   c) Gwaenynog Hall, Denbigh

3. **North Hoyle was Britain's first major offshore wind farm when it opened in 2003. It was built four miles off the coast of which town?**

   a) Prestatyn

   b) Aberystwyth

   c) Barry

4. **Which of the following former Manchester United players was named manager of the Wales national football team in January 2018?**

   a) Mark Hughes

   b) Mickey Thomas

   c) Ryan Giggs

5. In which year were women first allowed to become priests in the Church in Wales?

    a) 1987
    b) 1992
    c) 1997

6. In 1999, who became the inaugural First Secretary of the National Assembly of Wales, a position which was later renamed First Minister?

    a) John Marek
    b) Alun Michael
    c) Ron Davies

7. Robert Recorde's career included being a royal physician and controller of the Royal Mint. Which mathematical symbol did he introduce to the world in 1557?

    a) equals sign
    b) square root sign
    c) percentage sign

8. Ebbw Vale-born Brian Hibbard became famous in the early 1980s as a founding member of which a cappella group?

9. Laura Mountney was born on 7 September 1925 in Dowlais, Merthyr Tydfil. Which textile design business, floated on the stock market with a valuation of £200 million in 1986, did she establish with her husband Bernard?

10. In which film trilogy did John Rhys-Davies play the role of Gimli the dwarf?

Round 10

1. **Where did Walter de Clare build a Cistercian abbey in 1131?**
    a) Swansea
    b) Newport
    c) Tintern

2. **Launched in 1814, what was the first Welsh-language weekly newspaper?**
    a) *Y Barcud*
    b) *Seren Gomer*
    c) *Yr Arwydd*

3. **In which city was the Egypt Centre opened in 1998 as a museum of Egyptian antiquities?**
    a) Swansea
    b) St Asaph
    c) St Davids

4. **Which car manufacturer opened an engine production plant in Bridgend during May 1980?**
    a) Mazda
    b) Toyota
    c) Ford

5. **Surreal comedy *Satellite City* first aired in 1996. Who played the role of sharp-tongued Gwynne Price?**
    a) Rhodri Hugh
    b) Boyd Clack
    c) William Thomas

6. In football, who in 2011 became the Wales national side's youngest ever captain at 20 years and 90 days?

    a) Aaron Ramsey

    b) Joe Allen

    c) Chris Gunter

7. Isaac Roberts was an acclaimed pioneer of astrophotography. What was he the first person to take a photo of in December 1888?

    a) Hoag's Object

    b) Great Nebula in Andromeda

    c) The Southern Pinwheel

8. Iwan Rheon appeared in 20 episodes of Game of Thrones from 2013 until 2016. Which character did he play?

9. Who made his operatic debut in 1990 as Guglielmo in *Così Fan Tutte* for the Welsh National Opera, before beginning his international career in 1991 when he appeared as the speaker in *Die Zauberflöte*?

10. In which rowing event did Tom James earn Olympic gold in 2008 and 2012?

Round 11

1. **In which national park would you find the peaks of Carnedd Llewelyn and Glyder Fawr?**

   a) Brecon Beacons
   b) Snowdonia
   c) Pembrokeshire Coast

2. **The Second Severn Crossing was opened in 1996. The bridge took four years to build. How much did it cost?**

   a) £330 million
   b) £590 million
   c) £920 million

3. **The National Library of Wales was established in 1907. Where is it situated?**

   a) Machynlleth
   b) Cardiff
   c) Aberystwyth

4. **Who in 1955 was the last woman to be hanged in Britain, having been found guilty of shooting dead her violent partner David Blakely?**

   a) Muriel Clare
   b) Georgina Neilson
   c) Ruth Ellis

5. Which band's back catalogue includes the songs 'Guns Don't Kill People, Rappers Do' and 'Your Missus Is a Nutter'?

    a) Funeral for A Friend

    b) Goldie Lookin Chain

    c) Bullet for My Valentine

6. Hugh Griffith won a Best Supporting Actor Academy Award for his role in the 1959-released film *Ben Hur*. Which character did he play?

    a) Sheik Ilderim

    b) Messala

    c) Pontius Pilate

7. In 1218, Llywelyn the Great signed the Treaty of Worcester with which English king?

    a) Henry II

    b) Richard I

    c) Henry III

8. In which sport did 19-year old Jade Jones make history in 2012 by becoming the first British athlete to win Olympic gold in the discipline?

9. Which BBC programme did Huw Edwards present from 1999 until 2003?

10. Michael Howard was first elected to parliament in 1983. Which role did he hold in government from 1993 until 1997?

Round 12

1. **In which of the following towns would you find London Road, Briton Ferry Road and Dyfed Road?**
   a) Cwmbran
   b) Pontypool
   c) Neath

2. **Where was the Garth Pier opened in 1896?**
   a) Llandudno
   b) Bangor
   c) Penarth

3. **Which is the longest river that flows entirely through Wales?**
   a) Towy
   b) Teifi
   c) Dare

4. **In which 1954-released Alfred Hitchcock film did Ray Milland play the character Tony Wendice?**
   a) *Vertigo*
   b) *Strangers on a Train*
   c) *Dial M for Murder*

5. **Which English band collaborated with Cerys Matthews on the 1998-released single 'The Ballad of Tom Jones'?**
   a) Space
   b) Cast
   c) The Boo Radleys

6. Tony Award-winning actor Roger Rees made his name in the title role of the 1982 serialisation of *The Life and Adventures of Nicholas Nickelby*. In which American sitcom did he play the millionaire industrialist Robin Colcord from 1989 until 1993?

    a) *The Golden Girls*

    b) *Who's the Boss?*

    c) *Cheers*

7. In football, Wales defeated Russia 3-0 in Toulouse to reach the knockout stages of Euro 2016. Who scored his first international goal in the match?

    a) Ben Davies

    b) Neil Taylor

    c) Ashley Williams

8. Which Cardiff swimming pool, originally opened in 1958, was demolished in 1998?

9. Thomas Edward Lawrence was born on 16 August 1888 in Tremadog. Due to his influence on the Arab Revolt in the First World War, what was he better known as?

10. Where did Wrexham-born John Godfrey Parry-Thomas set a world land speed record of 171 miles per hour in April 1926?

Round 13

1. **Which of the following countries sits directly to the west of Wales?**

   a) Northern Ireland

   b) Republic of Ireland

   c) Iceland

2. **Which sport would you associate with Cliff Jones, Neville Southall and Ben Woodburn?**

   a) rugby union

   b) cricket

   c) football

3. **The Clwydian Range is a series of peaks in north-east Wales. What's the highest point within this area of outstanding natural beauty?**

   a) Moel Gyw

   b) Moel Fenlli

   c) Moel Famau

4. **In which of the following towns would you find the Ffwrnes Theatre?**

   a) Bridgend

   b) Llanelli

   c) Ammanford

5. **Which comedy panel show did the comedian Rob Brydon present for the first time in 2009?**

   a) *Would I Lie to You?*

   b) *8 Out of 10 Cats*

   c) *A League of Their Own*

6. **Ian Watkins and Lisa Scott-Lee released their first single with the band Steps in 1997 with the song '5, 6, 7, 8'. The track reached number 14 in the UK chart. What was the band's first top-ten single?**

   a) 'Last Thing on My Mind'
   b) 'One for Sorrow'
   c) 'Better Best Forgotten'

7. **Who played the role of Fatty Lewis in the 1997-released, Swansea-based black comedy film *Twin Town*?**

   a) Paul Durden
   b) Dorien Thomas
   c) Huw Ceredig

8. **Which 1983-released *Star Wars* film was directed by Richard Marquand?**

9. **Which male cyclist achieved gold for Wales in the road race at the 2014 Commonwealth Games in Glasgow?**

10. **Shakin' Stevens achieved four UK number one singles in the 1980s. Name them.**

Round 14

1. **Which of the following is a type of stew that usually contains ingredients such as lamb and leeks?**
    - a) Welsh rarebit
    - b) cawl
    - c) bara brith

2. **In which year did Wales introduce a minimum charge of five pence on single-use carrier bags?**
    - a) 2005
    - b) 2011
    - c) 2017

3. **Which type of boat was designed and built at Atlantic College, St Donat's during the 1960s?**
    - a) banana boat
    - b) kayak
    - c) rigid-hulled inflatable boat

4. **Who in 1920 became the first Archbishop of Wales after the Church in Wales was disestablished from the Church of England?**
    - a) Charles Green
    - b) David Prosser
    - c) Alfred George Edwards

5. **The comedy drama *Stella* first appeared on television in 2012. Which fictional location is it based in?**
    - a) Pontyberry
    - b) Fernvale
    - c) Tonyrhondda

6. **In 2005, 'Dakota' became the Stereophonics' first number one single. Which album was it from?**
   a) *Just Enough Education to Perform*
   b) *You Gotta Go There to Come Back*
   c) *Language. Sex. Violence. Other?*

7. **Ramsay MacDonald became the first Labour Prime Minister in 1924. Which constituency did he represent from 1922 until 1929?**
   a) Ceredigion
   b) Rhondda
   c) Aberavon

8. **Eglwys Rhos-born Harold Godfrey Lowe was the fifth officer on the infamous first voyage of which ship in 1912?**

9. **Who played Dylan Thomas in the 2008-released film *The Edge of Love*?**

10. **Which Cardiff department store, located on Queen Street, closed down on 8 September 1986?**

Round 15

1. **Which of the following mythological creatures is found on the Welsh flag?**

    a) phoenix

    b) centaur

    c) dragon

2. **Launched in 1974, what was Wales' first commercial radio station?**

    a) Heart Wales

    b) Swansea Sound

    c) Radio Maldwyn

3. **Which Cardiff cinema, situated on North Road, opened on 12 March 1928?**

    a) Plaza

    b) Gaiety Grand

    c) Avenue

4. **Which Academy Award-nominated film, released in 1999, tells the story of an orthodox Jew peddling fabrics door-to-door in the South Wales Valleys?**

    a) *Solomon & Gaenor*

    b) *Human Traffic*

    c) *House of America*

5. **With which band did Steve Strange achieve hit singles in the 1980s such as 'Fade to Grey', 'Mind of a Toy' and 'The Damned Don't Cry'?**

    a) Rich Kids

    b) Ultravox

    c) Visage

6. The 1978 film *Grand Slam* is about a group of Wales rugby fans travelling to Paris. Which character is played by Sion Probert?

   a) Mog Jones
   b) Maldwyn Pugh
   c) Caradog Lloyd-Evans

7. What did Dowlais Ironworks engineer Adrian Stephens invent in 1833 to prevent explosions in steam boilers?

   a) steam whistle
   b) double-disc pressure-release valve
   c) circular heat thermometer

8. What's the barrier between England and Wales, whose construction was ordered by the eighth-century King of Mercia, called?

9. What, in the grounds of Middleton Hall near Llanarthney, Carmarthenshire, was opened to the public in May 2000?

10. Nathan Cleverly became a boxing World Champion in 2011. In which subject did he earn a degree from Cardiff University the previous year?

Round 16

1. **Which of the following rivers flows through Llandysul and Llanybydder?**
   - a) Teifi
   - b) Gwili
   - c) Rheidol

2. **What's the most northerly town in Wales?**
   - a) Beaumaris
   - b) Holyhead
   - c) Amlwch

3. **Newtown entrepreneur Pryce Pryce-Jones patented the Euklisia Rug in 1876. This has been described as the world's first what?**
   - a) rubber floor tile
   - b) sleeping bag
   - c) toupee

4. **Gareth Bale's transfer from Tottenham Hotspur to Real Madrid in 2013 made him the second Welshman to achieve the status of world's most expensive footballer. Who was the first?**
   - a) John Charles
   - b) Trevor Ford
   - c) Ian Rush

5. **Christian Bale won the Best Actor Academy Award in 2011 for *The Fighter*. Where was he born?**

    a) Bangor

    b) Machynlleth

    c) Haverfordwest

6. **Gwynfor Evans became Plaid Cymru's first Member of Parliament in 1966. Which town's by-election did he win?**

    a) Carmarthen

    b) Llanelli

    c) Caernarfon

7. **In 2005, Gwyneth Lewis became the first person to hold which role?**

    a) Presiding Officer of the National Assembly for Wales

    b) Police and Crime Commissioner for Wales

    c) National Poet of Wales

8. **What property near Abergele was built by Lloyd Hesketh Bamford-Hesketh between 1812 and 1822 as a country house?**

9. ***The Goon Show* originally aired on the BBC Home Service from 1951 until 1960. Who was the Welshman starring with Peter Sellers and Spike Milligan in this comedy programme?**

10. **Which arts centre was opened in 1971 on the site of the former Canton High School in Cardiff?**

Round 17

1. **Which town launched a jazz festival in 1984, with George Melly as the headline act?**

   a) Builth Wells

   b) Denbigh

   c) Brecon

2. **Which waterfall near Llanrhaeadr-ym-Mochnant sits approximately 73 metres high in the Berwyn Mountains?**

   a) Aber Falls

   b) Pistyll Rhaeadr

   c) Conwy Falls

3. **What is awarded to the poet judged best in the free verse competition at the National Eisteddfod?**

   a) the Crown

   b) the Plate

   c) the Gold Chain

4. **Which of the following is a character in William Shakespeare's play _Henry VIII_?**

   a) Duke of Radnorshire

   b) Bishop of Llandaff

   c) Lord Abergavenny

5. **Jimmy Perry and David Croft's sitcom *Hi-de-Hi!* ran for 58 episodes from 1980 until 1988. Which character did Ruth Madoc play?**

    a) Peggy Ollerenshaw
    b) Gladys Pugh/Dempster
    c) Yvonne Stuart-Hargreaves

6. **Where did William Edwards build the then widest single-span bridge in Europe, completed in 1756?**

    a) Llawhaden
    b) Monmouth
    c) Pontypridd

7. **Which bank, founded in 1810, was known as 'The Black Sheep Bank' because its notes bore an engraving of one sheep for every pound represented?**

    a) Bala Bank
    b) Aberystwyth and Tregaron Bank
    c) Woods Bank

8. **World rankings were introduced into the sport of snooker in 1976. Who became the first ever world number one?**

9. **Which future English king captured Aberystwyth Castle from Owain Glyndŵr in 1408?**

10. *The procession returning from the fiesta of the Madonna Del Marco* **is considered the masterpiece of which nineteenth-century artist?**

Round 18

1. Desmond Llewelyn was most famous for his association with the James Bond film franchise. He first appeared as Boothroyd in *From Russia with Love*, a role which would in future be known as **Q**. How many of these movies did he appear in before his death in 1999?

   a) 7
   b) 12
   c) 17

2. Which of the following rivers flows through the town of Bridgend?

   a) Ogmore
   b) Taff
   c) Amman

3. In which town was a 72-foot high cast-iron clock tower erected in 1858, at a cost of approximately £1,000?

   a) Rhyl
   b) Pontypool
   c) Tredegar

4. Where in Cardiff during the first decade of the twentieth century is the first million-pound cheque considered to have been written?

   a) Norwegian Church
   b) Coal Exchange
   c) Cardiff Castle

5. **Who wrote *Aberystwyth Mon Amour*, the first in a series of spoof noir detective novels based on the character Louie Knight, the town's private investigator?**

   a) Cynan Jones
   b) Kate Roberts
   c) Malcolm Pryce

6. **In rugby union, which club defeated Australia 21-6 in 1992?**

   a) Swansea
   b) Neath
   c) Ebbw Vale

7. **Where was St David's College founded by Bishop Thomas Burgess in 1822?**

   a) Bangor
   b) Lampeter
   c) Wrexham

8. **Which BBC Radio 4 flagship programme did John Humphrys present for the first time in 1987?**

9. **Released in 1965, what was Tom Jones' first UK number one single?**

10. **Who was leader of the Labour Party from 1983 until 1992?**

Round 19

1. **In rugby union, which position would you associate with Barry John, Phil Bennett and Stephen Jones?**

   a) hooker

   b) flanker

   c) outside half

2. **In which town did the Dan Evans department store close in January 2006, after 100 years of trading?**

   a) Abergavenny

   b) Haverfordwest

   c) Barry

3. **Which of the following waterfalls is located on the River Teifi?**

   a) Cenarth Falls

   b) Sgwd yr Eira

   c) Henrhyd Falls

4. **The Royal Welsh Agricultural Society was formed in 1904. Which town held the first Royal Welsh Show in the same year?**

   a) Welshpool

   b) Aberystwyth

   c) Cowbridge

5. **Which future wife of Henry VIII was made Marquess of Pembroke in 1532, making her the most prestigious non-royal in the realm?**

   a) Anne Boleyn
   b) Catherine Howard
   c) Anne of Cleves

6. **On which road in Cardiff was the Gaiety Grand cinema, with its two art deco domes, opened in 1912?**

   a) Duke Street
   b) City Road
   c) Westgate Street

7. **In which year was the political party Plaid Cymru established?**

   a) 1907
   b) 1918
   c) 1925

8. **Which singer was born Gaynor Hopkins on 8 June 1951 in Skewen?**

9. **The film *Evita* was a musical drama released in 1996 depicting the life of Eva Perón, played by Madonna. Who portrayed her husband, Juan Perón?**

10. **Who, on 12 July 1910 during an air display at Hengistbury Airfield outside Bournemouth, became the first Briton to die in an aircraft accident?**

Round 20

1. **Which of the following places is <u>not</u> located in north Wales?**
   - a) St Mellons
   - b) Bethesda
   - c) Brymbo

2. **In which town did Hoover open a factory to produce washing machines in 1948?**
   - a) Pontypridd
   - b) Merthyr Tydfil
   - c) Aberdare

3. **Which of Snowdonia's mountains is famous for having twin monoliths on its summit known as Adam and Eve?**
   - a) Elidir Fawr
   - b) Tryfan
   - c) Glyder Fach

4. **In which town was a food festival launched by two farmers in 1999, in response to a lack of confidence by consumers in British produce?**
   - a) Knighton
   - b) Bala
   - c) Abergavenny

5. **Which brewery in the 1930s became the first outside the USA to commercially can beer?**
   - a) Brains
   - b) Buckley's
   - c) Felinfoel

6. **In which town was the Pont King Morgan cable-stayed footbridge opened in 2006?**

    a) Kidwelly
    b) Carmarthen
    c) Llandeilo

7. **Which musician's back catalogue includes songs such as 'The Sailor and Madonna', 'Ghost Town' and 'Ballad of Old Joe Blind'?**

    a) Meic Stevens
    b) Geraint Jarman
    c) Heather Jones

8. **Thomas Heslop, in 1814, was the last man to die in a duel in Wales. In which west Wales town, situated between Carmarthen and Cardigan, did he quarrel with his killer John Beynon in the Salutation Inn, resulting in the contest?**

9. **Which former Wales international footballer, known for his distinctive long blond hair during his playing days, appeared as a contestant on the BBC's 2011 series of *Strictly Come Dancing*?**

10. **What was the 1941 film set in Wales that won five Academy Awards, including Best Film (beating *Citizen Kane*) and Best Director?**

Round 21

1. **In which valley would you find Maerdy, Ferndale and Tylorstown?**
    a) Rhondda Fach
    b) Cynon
    c) Rhondda Fawr

2. ***Efrog Newydd* is the Welsh name for which American city?**
    a) Chicago
    b) San Francisco
    c) New York

3. **Which manuscript, a source of the Mabinogion tales, was presented to Jesus College, Oxford in 1701 by Reverend Thomas Wilkins of Llanbleddian?**
    a) *Red Book of Hergest*
    b) *White Book of Rhydderch*
    c) *Blue Book of Llwydiarth*

4. **In which year was Swansea granted city status?**
    a) 1929
    b) 1949
    c) 1969

5. **Who played the role of Gavin Kavanagh in the 2009-released, Richard Curtis-directed film *The Boat that Rocked*?**
    a) Andrew Howard
    b) Rhys Ifans
    c) Matthew Rhys

6. **Ricky Valance in August 1960 became the first Welshman to achieve a UK number one single. What was the song?**

        a) 'Jimmy's Girl'

        b) 'Tell Laura I Love Her'

        c) 'Moving Away'

7. **Which pair of brothers seized Conwy Castle on Good Friday 1401 while the garrison was at prayer, returning it to the crown two months later, gaining pardons for themselves while handing over some of their followers for execution?**

        a) Madog and Rhys ap Maredudd

        b) Hywel and Dafydd ap Gruffudd

        c) Rhys and Gwilym ap Tudur

8. **In boxing, at which weight have Howard Winstone, Steve Robinson and Lee Selby held world titles?**

9. **Shaheen Jafargholi reached the final of ITV's *Britain's Got Talent* in 2009. Which soap opera did he join in 2016, playing Bonnie Langford's son?**

10. **Who in 2002 became the first Welshman to be named Archbishop of Canterbury since the Reformation?**

Round 22

1. **Which of these places is situated on Wales' west coast?**
   - a) Aberaeron
   - b) Caldicot
   - c) Ruabon

2. **The A465 is a major road in south Wales. What's part of the road better known as?**
   - a) the Roman Motorway
   - b) the Heads of the Valleys Road
   - c) the Cattle Path

3. **In which town was a White Rabbit statue inspired by Lewis Carroll's classic book *Alice in Wonderland* unveiled in 1933?**
   - a) Rhyl
   - b) Mold
   - c) Llandudno

4. **In which year did Dilys Cadwaladr become the first woman to win the crown at the National Eisteddfod?**
   - a) 1937
   - b) 1953
   - c) 1978

5. **The first oxygen-blown integrated steelworks in Britain was opened by Queen Elizabeth II in 1962. Where was the site?**

   a) Llanwern
   b) Port Talbot
   c) Milford Haven

6. **Released on the Creation record label in 1996, *Fuzzy Logic* was the debut album by which band?**

   a) Super Furry Animals
   b) Feeder
   c) Catatonia

7. **Cardiff's Penarth Road Speedway Stadium was opened in 1951. It hosted both speedway and rugby league. When did it close?**

   a) 1953
   b) 1987
   c) 2005

8. **Langland Bay, Oxwich Point and Llangennith can all be found on which peninsula?**

9. **Which west Wales club side, known as The Drovers, won the Welsh Rugby Union Challenge Cup for the first time in their history with a two-point victory over Cardiff in 2007?**

10. ***How 2* was a fact-based children's programme that first aired in 1990. Who was the original co-host with Carol Vorderman and Fred Dinenage, remaining with the show for all 15 series?**

Round 23

1. **Aberdare is four miles to the south-west of which of the following towns?**
    a) Blackwood
    b) Merthyr Tydfil
    c) Pontypool

2. **Which sport is Major Walter Clopton Wingfield credited with inventing?**
    a) cricket
    b) golf
    c) lawn tennis

3. **The Welsh corgi is a small type of herding dog. There are two distinctive breeds. One is the Cardigan Welsh corgi. What's the other?**
    a) Glamorgan Welsh corgi
    b) Pembroke Welsh corgi
    c) Powys black

4. **Which town held its first International Musical Eisteddfod in 1947?**
    a) Llangollen
    b) Bodelwyddan
    c) Corwen

5. **The programme *Gladiators* was launched on ITV in 1992. Cardiff-born Aleks Georgijev was one of the original Gladiators. What was he known as?**

 a) Cobra
 b) Saracen
 c) Hawk

6. **Released in 1969, which song was Amen Corner's only UK number one single?**

 a) 'Hello Suzie'
 b) '(If Paradise Is) Half as Nice'
 c) 'Bend Me, Shape Me'

7. **Which of the following roles did Michael Heseltine hold from 1995 until 1997?**

 a) Deputy Prime Minister
 b) Chancellor of the Exchequer
 c) Secretary of State for Defence

8. **Which ground did Glamorgan County Cricket Club use for the first time while playing against a touring Indian side in May 1967?**

9. **Which castle was used for the investiture of a 20-year-old Prince Charles as Prince of Wales on 1 July 1969?**

10. **Who was awarded the 1950 Nobel Prize in literature 'in recognition of his varied and significant writings'?**

Round 24

1. **What percentage of Wales' inhabitants over the age of three had a knowledge of the Welsh language in 1991?**

    a) 14.2

    b) 18.5

    c) 27.1

2. **In which year was Owain Glyndŵr proclaimed Prince of Wales at Glyndyfrdwy?**

    a) 1352

    b) 1376

    c) 1400

3. **Which role in government was Labour MP Aneurin Bevan given in 1945?**

    a) Minister of Health

    b) Deputy Prime Minister

    c) Minister of Education

4. **Which two Welshmen were selected for the UEFA Euro 2016 Football Championship team of the tournament?**

    a) Joe Allen and Aaron Ramsey

    b) Gareth Bale and Ben Davies

    c) Ashley Williams and Joe Ledley

5. **What is the name of the twelfth-century Cistercian abbey located a mile from the village of Pontrhydfendigaid?**

    a) Valle Crucis

    b) St Dogmaels

    c) Strata Florida

6. **The Royal Mint initially relocated from Tower Hill in London to south Wales in 1968, before activity transferred fully in 1980. Where in south Wales was the chosen site?**

   a) Aberavon
   b) Bridgend
   c) Llantrisant

7. **Which Lordship was granted to Henry de Beaumont by Henry I in 1106?**

   a) Monmouth
   b) Gower
   c) Rhuddlan

8. **Which cave system in the Swansea Valley was discovered by the Morgan brothers in 1912?**

9. **Terry Cobner made 19 Test appearances for the Wales national rugby union side. Which club did he captain for a record ten seasons?**

10. **Who won British Academy of Film and Television Arts Best British Actress awards for her roles in *Saturday Night and Sunday Morning* and *This Sporting Life*?**

Round 25

1. **What did Caswell Bay and Little Haven become the first beaches in Wales to ban in 2016?**

    a) dog walking

    b) smoking

    c) metal detectors

2. **In which town would you find Ross Road, Hereford Road and Belgrave Road?**

    a) Colwyn Bay

    b) Cardigan

    c) Abergavenny

3. **Which of the following was Wales' first comprehensive school when it opened its doors in 1949?**

    a) Holyhead County School

    b) Porthcawl Comprehensive School

    c) Whitchurch High School

4. **In which year was a lido originally built at Ynysangharad Park in Pontypridd?**

    a) 1886

    b) 1902

    c) 1927

5. **Born in 1806, George Cornewall Lewis held government positions including Chancellor of the Exchequer and Home Secretary. Which Powys village erected the Lewis Monument in 1864 to remember this statesman?**

    a) New Radnor

    b) Llangors

    c) Abermule

6. The world's highest point above sea level, located on the border between Tibet and Nepal in the Himalayas, was named after Welshman George Everest in 1865. Which of the following positions did he <u>not</u> hold?

   a) Surveyor General of India
   b) Member of Parliament for Monmouth
   c) Vice President of the Royal Geographical Society

7. Which playwright's work included *Night Must Fall*, *A Murder Has Been Arranged* and *The Corn Is Green*?

   a) Norah Isaac
   b) Caradoc Evans
   c) Emlyn Williams

8. Which 1960s cult television series starring Patrick McGoohan was filmed at Portmeirion in north-west Wales?

9. Which Cardiff-born singer and guitarist achieved a solo UK Christmas number one hit in 1970 with the song 'I Hear You Knocking'?

10. The Walt Disney film *Mary Poppins*, starring Julie Andrews and Dick Van Dyke, was released in 1964. Which character was played by Glynis Johns?

Round 26

1. **The town of Maesteg sits on the banks of which river?**

    a) Afan

    b) Ely

    c) Llynfi

2. **Which town saw the Pugh Brothers department store close its doors for the last time in 2004?**

    a) Llanelli

    b) Pontypridd

    c) Bridgend

3. **In which year was the Dragon 32 microcomputer, produced by Port Talbot-based company Dragon Data Ltd, launched?**

    a) 1982

    b) 1988

    c) 1994

4. **Who in 1951, with a time of 13 hours and 55 minutes, became the first Welsh person to swim the English Channel?**

    a) Jean Foster

    b) John Brockway

    c) Jenny James

5. In 1996, which district in **Gwynedd** became the last area in **Wales** to remove the ban on the sale of alcohol on a **Sunday?**

    a) Arfon
    b) Meirionnydd
    c) Dwyfor

6. Launched on 25 April 1935, what was the name of the airline company based at **Pengam Moors airfield** to the east of **Cardiff?**

    a) Air Wales
    b) Cambrian Air Service
    c) South Wales Airways

7. Businessman **John Gronow** launched **Walesinabottle. com** in **September 2005.** What was the product being sold?

    a) water
    b) air
    c) memories

8. Which **MP,** first elected in 1945 for **Cardiff South,** was **UK Prime Minister from 1976 until 1979?**

9. Who, with two goals, was **Wales'** highest goal scorer at the **1958 FIFA football World Cup Finals** in **Sweden?**

10. Which youth organisation was launched in 1922 by **Ifan ab Owen Edwards?**

Round 27

1. **How many seats were won by the Liberal Democrats from the 40 available Welsh constituencies in the 1997 UK General Election?**

    a) 2
    b) 7
    c) 11

2. **In which year was Newport given city status?**

    a) 1976
    b) 1991
    c) 2002

3. **Through which of the following towns does the Arlais Brook flow?**

    a) Caerphilly
    b) Pwllheli
    c) Llandrindod Wells

4. **Radio 1 DJ Huw Stephens co-founded the Sŵn music festival. Which city hosted the inaugural event in 2007?**

    a) Bangor
    b) Cardiff
    c) Swansea

5. **Cardiff-born Jamie Shaw was successfully selected to become a member of a pop group in the 2002 ITV series *Popstars: The Rivals*. What was the band called?**

    a) Busted
    b) Liberty X
    c) One True Voice

6. **On which river did Thomas Telford design a weir called Horseshoe Falls to collect water for the Llangollen Canal?**

    a) Dee

    b) Conwy

    c) Dovey

7. **Godfrey Morgan, Viscount Tredegar, commanded a squadron of the 17th Regiment of Light Dragoons during the Charge of the Light Brigade in 1854. Which country's forces were the opposition?**

    a) Spain

    b) Russia

    c) Greece

8. **'Come and Get It', 'No Matter What' and 'Day after Day' were hit singles released by which band between 1969 and 1971?**

9. **Which Tonypandy-born actor appeared in television programmes such as *Keep It in the Family*, *The Long Chase* and *A Horseman Riding By*?**

10. **Approximately 100,000 people took to the streets of Cardiff in 1925 to pay their respects on the passing of the 44-year-old landlord of the Duke of Edinburgh pub. Wales had never previously seen a funeral of such a size. Which world-famous former boxer had died?**

Round 28

1. **Which part of Wales has a meat-free sausage consisting of ingredients such as cheese, leeks, herbs and breadcrumbs named after it?**
    a) Glamorgan
    b) Gwynedd
    c) Clwyd

2. **Snowdon is the highest mountain in Wales. How high is its peak?**
    a) 973 metres
    b) 1,085 metres
    c) 1,143 metres

3. **The first vote on the limited devolution of Wales from the United Kingdom took place on 1 March 1979. In it, 956,330 people voted against devolution. How many supported the proposal?**
    a) 171,524
    b) 243,048
    c) 312,601

4. **In which year was BBC Wales launched, providing five hours of English-language television and seven hours of Welsh-language television per week?**
    a) 1964
    b) 1967
    c) 1971

5. **Which country in 1872 had 384 Welsh-language chapels?**
   a) Australia
   b) England
   c) United States of America

6. **23 June 1894 is a day etched in the history of Cilfynydd, as a mining disaster killed 290 men and boys. What was the name of the colliery involved?**
   a) Tynewydd Colliery
   b) Prince of Wales Pit
   c) Albion Colliery

7. **Julien MacDonald was born in Merthyr Tydfil, where his mother taught him how to knit from an early age. Which Paris couture house appointed him chief designer in 2001?**
   a) Givenchy
   b) Chanel
   c) Christian Dior

8. **Colwyn Bay-born Paula Yates died in 2000 at the age of 41. Which Channel 4 programme, launched in 1982, did she co-present with Jools Holland?**

9. **In 1995, which BBC Middle East correspondent won the Best News Correspondent award at the New York Television Festival?**

10. **In football, who won a record 13th Premier League title with Manchester United in 2013?**

Round 29

1. **Which of the following bodies of water is located to the south of Wales?**
    a) Sea of the Hebrides
    b) Moray Firth
    c) Bristol Channel

2. **The first Roman gold mine to be discovered in the UK is at Dolaucothi. Which town is located 5 miles south-east of this location?**
    a) Llandovery
    b) Bala
    c) Port Talbot

3. **The record for the world's longest line of drinks cans was set at Bridgend recreation centre in 2009. How many cans were used?**
    a) 33,482
    b) 76,129
    c) 106,300

4. **Which town's industrial landscape was designated a UNESCO World Heritage Site in the year 2000?**
    a) Pontypool
    b) Blaenavon
    c) Merthyr Tydfil

5. **What's the name of the fictional fishing village in Dylan Thomas' 'play for voices' *Under Milk Wood*?**
    a) Llareggub
    b) Aberdimbyd
    c) Caeroma

6. **In 1998, which Manic Street Preachers song became their first UK number 1 single?**

    a) 'If You Tolerate This Your Children Will Be Next'
    b) 'A Design for Life'
    c) 'Australia'

7. **In which 1990s comedy series did Kevin Allen play the role of Detective Constable Robert Kray?**

    a) *Father Ted*
    b) *The Thin Blue Line*
    c) *Bottom*

8. **Clothes designer Jeff Banks was one of the original co-presenters of which BBC fashion programme when it was launched in October 1986?**

9. **In football, Liverpool defeated Club Brugge over two legs in the 1976 UEFA Cup final with an aggregate score of 4-3. Which two Welshmen gained winners' medals?**

10. **The £20 million Pont Briwet bridge was completed in 2015, replacing a 150-year-old wooden structure. Which estuary does it cross?**

Round 30

1. **Which sport would you associate with Brian Huggett, Dai Rees, Ian Woosnam and Bradley Dredge?**

   a) golf

   b) cricket

   c) motor racing

2. **Who played the role of Just Judy in the Christmas-themed romantic-comedy film _Love Actually_?**

   a) Joanna Page

   b) Eve Myles

   c) Rhian Blythe

3. **Cardiff-born Donna Lewis achieved a US Billboard Dance Club chart number one hit in 1998. What was the song?**

   a) 'I Love You Always Forever'

   b) 'Without Love'

   c) 'Love Him'

4. **In 1778, John Morris installed the largest pump in the world into Pentre Pit coal mine to combat flooding. How many gallons of water per hour could the pump remove?**

   a) 5,000

   b) 31,000

   c) 72,000

5. **Which two colours were used on Owain Glyndŵr's four lions rampant flag?**

   a) red and gold
   b) green and white
   c) gold and black

6. **Who played the role of Private Owen in the 1964 film *Zulu*?**

   a) Ray Milland
   b) Gareth Thomas
   c) Ivor Emmanuel

7. **Which reality television programme did Llanelli's Sam Evans win in 2013?**

   a) *The Bachelor*
   b) *Big Brother*
   c) *Britain's Got Talent*

8. **Which car manufacturer, founded by master butcher Giles Smith and engineer Bernard Friese, set up a factory in Llantwit Fardre in 1961?**

9. **Which artist created the cover illustrations for Super Furry Animals' albums *Radiator* and *Mwng*?**

10. **Which financial services group was founded by Henry Englehardt in Cardiff in 1993?**

Round 31

1. **According to the 2011 census, what percentage of residents in Wales considered their religion to be Christianity?**
   - a) 44%
   - b) 58%
   - c) 72%

2. **In which town was the Prince Charles Hospital opened in 1978?**
   - a) Newtown
   - b) Queensferry
   - c) Merthyr Tydfil

3. **In which year did the Welsh-language soap opera *Pobol y Cwm* first make an appearance on BBC One?**
   - a) 1964
   - b) 1969
   - c) 1974

4. **Margaret John appeared in programmes such as *Z Cars* and *Doctor Who* during the 1970s. Which role did she play in the comedy series *Gavin and Stacey*?**
   - a) Doris
   - b) Betty
   - c) Marjorie

5. Which town is associated with a Black Book, reputedly written at its priory in the thirteenth century, making it one of the oldest surviving manuscripts in the Welsh language?

      a) Neath

      b) Carmarthen

      c) Pwllheli

6. On 27 April 1939, the horse Grasshopper won the last race held at which Cardiff racecourse?

      a) Ely

      b) Maindy

      c) Grangetown

7. In which cycling event did Elinor Barker win Olympic gold at the Rio 2016 Games?

      a) keirin

      b) team pursuit

      c) omnium

8. Which three James Bond films, released during the 1960s and 1970s, had theme songs sung by Shirley Bassey?

9. George Thomas was first elected to Parliament in 1945, becoming Viscount Tonypandy in 1983. What role did he occupy in the House of Commons from 1976 until 1983?

10. Which Cardiff-based sci-fi drama, first aired in 2006, included the characters Captain Jack Harkness, Gwen Cooper and Ianto Jones?

Round 32

1. **On which Welsh coast would you find the town of Prestatyn?**
   a) north
   b) west
   c) south

2. **In 1983, which BBC-organised competition did Finnish soprano Karita Mattila become the first person to win?**
   a) Wales Operatic Eisteddfod
   b) Cardiff Singer of the World
   c) St Asaph Music Night

3. **Arthur Whitten Brown made the first successful non-stop transatlantic flight in June 1919 with John Alcock. Where did he die in 1948, having lived there for 25 years?**
   a) Bangor
   b) Cardiff
   c) Swansea

4. **Which micro-brewery based in Porthmadog was launched in 2005 with a one-off special pale ale called No.1?**
   a) Crafty Devil
   b) Purple Moose
   c) Tiny Rebel

5. **In which area of Swansea was the John Humphrey-designed Tabernacle chapel completed in 1872 at a staggering cost of £18,000?**

    a) Sketty

    b) Fforestfach

    c) Morriston

6. **In which year did Miss Wales Rosemarie Frankland become Britain's first Miss World?**

    a) 1961

    b) 1968

    c) 1975

7. **Which is the sole remaining mediaeval fortified river bridge in Britain where the gate tower stands on the bridge?**

    a) Crickhowell Bridge

    b) Llawhaden Bridge

    c) Monnow Bridge

8. **Which island in the Bristol Channel had a traffic light system installed in 2014 to prevent people from getting trapped when the tide comes in, covering the rocky causeway?**

9. **Carmarthen-born Rob Wainwright was appointed Executive Director of which security institution in 2009?**

10. **Who wrote The Man from U.N.C.L.E. books, *The Copenhagen Affair* and *The Stone-Cold Dead in The Market Affair*?**

Round 33

1. **What's the name of the large bay that runs down the west coast of Wales from Bardsey Island in the north to Strumble Head in the south?**
   a) Cardigan Bay
   b) Carmarthen Bay
   c) New Quay Bay

2. **In which year was 'pay at the pump' first introduced to fuel stations in Wales as a method of paying to fill your vehicle?**
   a) 1984
   b) 1994
   c) 2004

3. **In 1857, which town was given a cannon used during the Charge of the Light Brigade, in memory of its soldiers' sacrifices in the Crimean War?**
   a) Whitland
   b) Tenby
   c) Cardigan

4. **The Hengoed Viaduct was constructed during the 1850s with 16 arches, each 40 feet in span. Which river does it cross?**
   a) Rhymney
   b) Taff
   c) Sirhowy

5. Which rugby union player teamed up with folk singer Maralene Powell in 1972 to top the Welsh-language charts with the song *Wyt Ti Weithiau?*?

   a) Barry John
   b) Gareth Edwards
   c) Gerald Davies

6. What was the name of the ship that left Cardiff in 1910 to transport Captain Robert Falcon Scott's team to the South Pole?

   a) *Manx Maid*
   b) *Rifleman*
   c) *Terra Nova*

7. In which comedy series, first aired in 1974, did Windsor Davies play the role of Battery Sergeant Major 'Shut Up' Williams?

   a) *Bless This House*
   b) *It Ain't Half Hot Mum*
   c) *Dad's Army*

8. Which Labour politician held the role of First Minister of Wales from 2000 until 2009?

9. Barry-born Mike Young created *SuperTed* as a bedtime story for his stepson, before turning it into an animated series. Which star of *Doctor Who* and *Worzel Gummidge* provided the voice for the character Spotty in the English version of the cartoon during the 1980s?

10. In rugby union, Adam Jones made his 95th appearance for Wales in June 2014. Which position did he play?

Round 34

1. **Which of the following rivers flows through Cardiff?**

   a) Wye

   b) Taff

   c) Elwy

2. **In which year was the National Museum of Wales incorporated by royal charter?**

   a) 1856

   b) 1879

   c) 1907

3. **For which 1993-released film did Anthony Hopkins receive a Best Actor Academy Award nomination for his portrayal of butler James Stevens?**

   a) *The Remains of the Day*

   b) *Legends of the Fall*

   c) *Desperate Hours*

4. **Neil Hamilton was Conservative MP for Tatton from 1983 until 1997. In 2016, he was elected as a Member of the Welsh Assembly. Which political party did he represent?**

   a) Labour

   b) Liberal Democrats

   c) UK Independence Party

5. **Who achieved a French number one hit in 2003 with the song '*Si Demain*'?**

   a) Katherine Jenkins
   b) Bonnie Tyler
   c) Andy Fairweather Low

6. **Charles, Prince of Wales married Lady Diana Spencer on 29 July 1981 at St Paul's Cathedral, London. Who designed the bride's dress?**

   a) Laura Ashley
   b) Jeff Banks
   c) David and Elizabeth Emanuel

7. **David Edward Hughes started his career as an inventor when he patented a printing type telegraph instrument in 1855. What did he devise in 1878?**

   a) ballpoint pen
   b) hydraulic press
   c) carbon microphone

8. **Francis Lewis was born on 21 March 1713 in Llandaff, and sailed to New York in the 1730s. Which significant document in the history of the United States of America was he a signatory of in 1776?**

9. **Which 1978 Ian Dury & The Blockheads number one single's lyrics included the line 'In the dock of Tiger Bay'?**

10. **In rugby union, which club supplied 20 of the first 60 players to have captained the Welsh national side?**

Round 35

1. **Abersoch, Aberdaron and Tudweiliog are places located on which peninsula?**

   a) Shell Island
   b) Llŷn Peninsula
   c) Gower Peninsula

2. **The Preseli Mountains are a series of hills located in the northern part of which county?**

   a) Pembrokeshire
   b) Flintshire
   c) Powys

3. **Neath-born Ray Milland became the first Welshman to earn an Academy Award, winning the Best Actor Oscar for his role as the character Don Birnam. Which 1945-released film was this in?**

   a) *A Tree Grows in Brooklyn*
   b) *The Treasure of the Sierra Madre*
   c) *The Lost Weekend*

4. **Which sport would you associate with Cliff Morgan, Ieuan Evans, Neil Jenkins and Leigh Halfpenny?**

   a) rugby union
   b) cricket
   c) darts

5. The Britannia Bridge crossing the Menai Strait was originally completed in March 1850. In which year was it almost totally destroyed by fire?

    a) 1913
    b) 1951
    c) 1970

6. In which year did Lucie Jones from Pentyrch, representing the UK, finish 15th in the Eurovision Song Contest with 'Never Give Up on You'?

    a) 2009
    b) 2013
    c) 2017

7. What trophy is awarded to the successful bard for the best long poem at the National Eisteddfod?

    a) the Medal
    b) the Chair
    c) the Bowl

8. In which conflict did Welsh Guardsman Simon Weston receive 46% burns as his ship, the *Sir Galahad*, was destroyed at Bluff Cove in 1982?

9. Which bestselling author's back catalogue of spy genre books includes *Snow Falcon*, *Sea Leopard* and *Jade Tiger*?

10. In football, which former Denmark international managed Swansea City to a 5-0 victory over Bradford City in the 2013 Football League Cup final?

Round 36

1. **Craig Goch and Pen-y-Garreg dams are located on which mid-Wales river?**

   a) Claerwen

   b) Elan

   c) Ystwyth

2. **In rugby union, which of the following clubs did Wales internationals Iestyn Thomas, Byron Hayward and Kingsley Jones all play for?**

   a) Cardiff

   b) Ebbw Vale

   c) Swansea

3. **Henry Richard was appointed Secretary of the Peace Society in 1848. Which town's square has a statue to commemorate him?**

   a) Tregaron

   b) Aberaeron

   c) Llandeilo

4. **In 1856, father and son duo Evan and James wrote the words and composed the music respectively to the Welsh national anthem *'Hen Wlad Fy Nhadau'*. What was their surname?**

   a) Llewellyn

   b) Parry

   c) James

5. **Which modern-day town sits on the site of the Roman fortress Isca Silurum?**

    a) Caerleon

    b) Neath

    c) Bridgend

6. **Where was the re-launched National Wool Museum established in 2004?**

    a) Llanidloes

    b) Pwllheli

    c) Drefach Felindre

7. **Lieutenant-General Thomas Picton was the most senior British officer to die at the Battle of Waterloo. Which island was he previously the governor of for five years from 1797?**

    a) Jamaica

    b) Trinidad

    c) Australia

8. **The British Academy of Songwriters, Composers and Authors celebrate excellence with a yearly awards ceremony. Which Cardiff-born composer and actor are the awards named after?**

9. **Which band's back catalogue includes hit songs such as 'Gimme Some Lovin'', 'I'm a Man' and 'Keep on Running'?**

10. **Who portrayed David Frost in the 2008 historical drama film *Frost/Nixon*?**

Round 37

1. **Laverbread is made from which of the following ingredients?**
   - a) seaweed
   - b) curly kale
   - c) rye

2. **Which world-famous soprano made Craig-y-Nos Castle near Ystradgynlais her home in 1878?**
   - a) Nellie Melba
   - b) Adelina Patti
   - c) Eugenia Tadolini

3. **Which sport would you associate with Dominic Dale, Mark Williams, Matthew Stevens and Ryan Day?**
   - a) horse racing
   - b) basketball
   - c) snooker

4. **Sam Wakeling set a world record at Aberystwyth University in 2007 for the longest distance travelled on a unicycle in 24 hours. How many miles did he travel?**
   - a) 156.30
   - b) 239.15
   - c) 281.85

5. **Senghennydd was the scene of Britain's worst mining disaster on 14 October 1913. How many miners were tragically killed?**
   - a) 312
   - b) 387
   - c) 439

6. **In which American state would you find the township of Lower Gwynedd?**

    a) Pennsylvania
    b) Alabama
    c) Minnesota

7. **Carol Vorderman was the first woman to appear on Channel 4 when *Countdown* launched the network in 1982. For how many consecutive years did she co-present the show?**

    a) 22
    b) 26
    c) 32

8. **Which Cardiff-born singer became the youngest artist to top the UK classical chart with the 1998-released album *Voice of an Angel*?**

9. **Michael Foot was Labour Party leader from 1980 until 1983. Who did he succeed as MP for Ebbw Vale in 1960?**

10. **Richard Burton never won an Academy Award, even though he was nominated on numerous occasions. How many nominations did he receive?**

Round 38

1. **Which of the following places is regarded as the gateway to the Rhondda, as the valleys of the Rhondda Fawr and Rhondda Fach rivers meet there?**
   a) Tonypandy
   b) Treorchy
   c) Porth

2. **The Pontcysyllte Aquaduct was completed in 1805. It stands 38 metres above the River Dee. How long is it?**
   a) 204 metres
   b) 271 metres
   c) 307 metres

3. **In which year was the Canton Cinema on Cowbridge Road in Cardiff opened?**
   a) 1887
   b) 1914
   c) 1959

4. **Who was the Prince of Dyfed in the first branch of the *Mabinogion*?**
   a) Pwyll
   b) Gwydion
   c) Mathonwy

5. **Who went on air as the first *BBC Wales Today* news presenter in September 1962?**
   a) Vincent Kane
   b) Brian Hoey
   c) David Parry-Jones

6. **Newport-born computer programmer Adam Powell co-founded and launched which of the following websites in 1999?**

    a) Neopets
    b) Moshi Monsters
    c) The Sims

7. **In football, which accolade did Gareth Bale receive while playing for Tottenham Hotspur in 2013, which had previously been received by Everton's Neville Southall in 1985 and Liverpool's Ian Rush in 1984?**

    a) BBC Sports Personality of the Year
    b) Football Writers' Association Footballer of the Year
    c) Inductee to the Welsh Sports Hall of Fame

8. **Who wrote a bestselling memoir called *Mr Nice*, released in 1996, a year after his release from prison in the USA, where he'd been incarcerated for drug offences?**

9. **Which town did the Arthurian wizard Merlin apparently prophesy would fall if an old oak standing in it (till 1978) should tumble?**

10. **In which Cardiff park will you find a statue of Billy the Seal?**

Round 39

1. **Which of these bodies of water is located to the west of Wales?**
    a) Baltic Sea
    b) Irish Sea
    c) Torres Strait

2. **Poet Dylan Thomas was born in Swansea in 1914. Where was he buried, in the churchyard of St Martin's Church, following his death in 1953?**
    a) Laugharne
    b) Penarth
    c) Beddgelert

3. **Which Welsh businessman developed the Celtic Manor Resort near Newport into a venue that hosted the 2010 Ryder Cup and a 2014 NATO summit?**
    a) David Sullivan
    b) Steve Morgan
    c) Terry Matthews

4. **William Robert Grove was a scientist and judge who, in 1839, invented the Grove Cell, a step towards the modern battery. Where was he born, in 1811?**
    a) Llandudno
    b) Newbridge
    c) Swansea

5. In rugby union, which country did **Cardiff** defeat 8-3 in 1953, with tries by **Sid Judd** and **Gwyn Rowlands**?

   a) New Zealand
   b) South Africa
   c) Scotland

6. Which town in the 1850s erected a monument shaped like an upturned cannon, as a memorial to the Duke of Wellington and his victory at the Battle of Waterloo?

   a) Pontypool
   b) Aberystwyth
   c) Porthmadog

7. Where was **Llywelyn ap Gruffydd**, the last Prince of Wales, killed by one of **Edward I**'s soldiers in 1282?

   a) Cilmeri
   b) Knighton
   c) Llanwrtyd Wells

8. Which band, formed on the television programme *Popstars* and including Cardiff-born **Noel Sullivan**, reached number one in the UK charts in 2001 with the single 'Pure and Simple'?

9. Who was the National Assembly for Wales' Presiding Officer from 1999 until 2011?

10. For which 2002-released film did **Catherine Zeta-Jones** win an Academy Award for Best Actress in a Supporting Role?

Round 40

1. **In which film franchise did John Rhys-Davies make his first appearance as Sallah, 'the best digger in Egypt', in 1981?**
   a) *James Bond*
   b) *Indiana Jones*
   c) *Star Trek*

2. **Which political party was Montgomeryshire MP Clement Davies the leader of from 1945 until 1956?**
   a) Liberal Party
   b) Green Party
   c) Labour Party

3. **In which year was Cardiff made capital of Wales?**
   a) 1857
   b) 1911
   c) 1955

4. **What was the name of the ship that in 1865 took the first group of Welsh settlers to a new colony in Patagonia?**
   a) *White Dove*
   b) *Mimosa*
   c) *Olympus*

5. **Who in 2016 won the 74th edition of the Paris–Nice road cycling stage race?**
   a) Geraint Thomas
   b) Luke Rowe
   c) Owain Doull

6. **Of the first six Presidents of the USA, how many were of Welsh descent?**

    a) four

    b) five

    c) six

7. **In 1985, Aled Jones reached number five in the UK charts with 'Walking in the Air'. Which television programme did he co-host from 2012 until 2014?**

    a) *Homes under the Hammer*

    b) *Crimewatch*

    c) *Daybreak*

8. **Which Pembrokeshire-born former champion steeplechase jockey became an international bestselling author of over 40 crime novels including *Blood Sport*, *Whip Hand* and *Come to Grief*?**

9. **Which Stanleytown-born comedian, actor and writer is best known for his work on sketch shows such as *The Fast Show*, *Harry Enfield and Chums* and *Harry & Paul*?**

10. **Released in 2008, what was Duffy's first UK number one single?**

Round 41

1. In which sport have Howard Winstone, Barry Jones, Gavin Rees and Enzo Maccarinelli been world champions?

   a) squash

   b) tennis

   c) boxing

2. Which of the following towns hosted its first Festival of Literature and Arts in 1988?

   a) Ebbw Vale

   b) Monmouth

   c) Hay-on-Wye

3. In which town was Christ College founded as a modern public school by an Act of Parliament in 1855, after coming into being under a Royal Charter from Henry VIII in 1541?

   a) Brecon

   b) Lampeter

   c) Bridgend

4. In which year did Cardiff host the British Empire and Commonwealth Games?

   a) 1950

   b) 1954

   c) 1958

5. **Which band's back catalogue of albums includes *Patio*, *Bwyd Time* and *Spanish Dance Troupe*?**

   a) Topper

   b) Gorky's Zygotic Mynci

   c) Big Leaves

6. **Which of the following actors appeared in the Beatles films *A Hard Day's Night*, *Help!* and *Magical Mystery Tour*?**

   a) Victor Spinetti

   b) Ray Smith

   c) Hubert Rees

7. **Treorchy-born Donald Davies was a computing pioneer who had a major effect on the development of the internet. What data-sharing process did he develop?**

   a) File Transfer Protocol

   b) packet sharing

   c) network file sharing

8. ***Forever* was an American fantasy crime drama television series, first aired in 2014, about a man cursed with immortality. Who played the starring role of Doctor Henry Morgan?**

9. **Who in 1929, representing the Liberal Party, became the first female MP from Wales?**

10. **Which peninsula became the UK's first officially designated Area of Outstanding Beauty in 1956?**

Round 42

1. **The town of Tredegar sits within which river's valley?**
    a) Dee
    b) Cleddau
    c) Sirhowy

2. **Which of the following peaks is 1,064 metres in elevation?**
    a) Moel Hebog
    b) Carnedd Llewelyn
    c) Glyder Fawr

3. **The band Scritti Politti was formed in 1977 by which Cardiff-born frontman?**
    a) Green Gartside
    b) Andy Fairweather Low
    c) Dave Edmunds

4. **On 22 September 1934 an explosion at a north Wales mine resulted in 266 deaths. Which colliery was the scene of this disaster?**
    a) Gresford
    b) Hafod
    c) Llay Hall

5. **Newborough Forest was planted with Corsican pine trees between 1947 and 1965 to protect the village of Newborough from wind-blown sand and to stabilise sand dunes. Where in Wales is it located?**
    a) Pembrokeshire
    b) Anglesey
    c) Powys

6. Bill Frost is said to have flown 500 yards before crashing in September 1896 – seven years before the Wright brothers, who are commonly credited as the first men to fly a power-driven aeroplane. There is no written evidence of this, but there is evidence that he patented a flying machine two years earlier. What was his day job?

    a) butcher

    b) fisherman

    c) carpenter

7. Who became the first Secretary of State for Wales, in 1964?

    a) Jim Griffiths

    b) Leo Abse

    c) Cledwyn Hughes

8. The Oliver Stone-directed biographical film *Nixon* was released in 1995. Who played the role of Richard Nixon?

9. In football, who in 1973 transferred from Leeds United to Birmingham City for £100,000, a world record transfer fee for a goalkeeper at the time?

10. John Hughes started a ceramics business from his garden shed in 1965. What did the figures he produced become known as?

Round 43

1. **In which year was the television channel S4C launched?**

    a) 1982

    b) 1984

    c) 1986

2. **Which James Bond actor, who starred in both *The Living Daylights* and *Licence to Kill*, was born in Colwyn Bay?**

    a) Pierce Brosnan

    b) Timothy Dalton

    c) Daniel Craig

3. **Where would you find the remote, slightly curved, sandy beach named Barafundle Bay?**

    a) Gwynedd

    b) Ceredigion

    c) Pembrokeshire

4. **Reginald George Lewis was the youngest recorded Welsh casualty of World War I when he died at the age of 14 on 6 August 1918. Where was he from?**

    a) Barry

    b) Llanddeusant

    c) Narberth

5. **Richard Steele was a writer, playwright and politician. He was buried at St Peter's church in Carmarthen in 1729. Which magazine did he establish in 1709?**

   a) *The Gentleman's Magazine*

   b) *The Town and Country Magazine*

   c) *The Tatler*

6. **The first grandstand built at Cardiff's Arms Park recreational sports ground in 1881 had 300 seats 'for the convenience of the spectators and ladies in particular'. How much did it cost to build?**

   a) £50.00

   b) £250.00

   c) £375.00

7. **What's the prominent limestone headland rising 207 metres out of the sea next to Llandudno called?**

   a) Y Garn

   b) Moel Siabod

   c) Great Orme

8. **The children's television programme *Fireman Sam* was first aired in 1987. What is the name of the fictional village where it's based?**

9. **Which brewery was built by David John on the outskirts of Llanelli in 1878?**

10. **On 2 June 1910, who became the first person to make a non-stop flight from England to France then back again?**

Round 44

1. Which of the following is <u>not</u> found on the Gower Peninsula?

    a) Oxwich Bay

    b) Rhossili Bay

    c) Rest Bay

2. Which of the following waterfalls is located to the south-east of Machynlleth?

    a) Conwy Falls

    b) Pistyll y Llyn

    c) Pwll-y-Wrach

3. With which group did Nicky Stevens win the 1976 Eurovision Song Contest with the song 'Save Your Kisses for Me'?

    a) Brotherhood of Man

    b) Co-Co

    c) Bucks Fizz

4. Cardiff's Capitol Theatre was opened in December 1921 as the largest purpose-built cinema in Europe. In which year was it demolished?

    a) 1961

    b) 1972

    c) 1983

5. The Pembrokeshire Coast Path twists and turns its way through breathtaking coastal scenery. How long is it?

    a) 43 miles

    b) 97 miles

    c) 186 miles

6. Which castle in 1401 was the scene of the gruesome killing of Llywelyn ap Gruffudd Fychan, a leading squire and supporter of Owain Glyndŵr, by Henry IV?

     a) Llandovery
     b) Dinefwr
     c) Dryslwyn

7. Which of the following artists reached number one in the UK album chart in 1975 with *We All Had Doctors' Papers*?

     a) Frank Hennessy
     b) Max Boyce
     c) Meic Stevens

8. In rugby union, Wales defeated Scotland 17-3 at Murrayfield in 1969. Who won the first of his 55 caps for his country in the match?

9. Which country elected Welsh-speaking Billy Hughes as Prime Minister in 1915?

10. Which theatre director's back catalogue of work includes a production of *Bent* at the National Theatre, London in 1990, *Waiting for Godot* at the Theatre Royal Haymarket, London in 2009 and *No Man's Land* at Berkeley Repertory Theatre, California in 2013?

Round 45

1. **Which of the following is a small round boat made of wickerwork covered with a watertight material and propelled with a paddle?**

    a) gondola

    b) dory

    c) coracle

2. **Legend has it that Prince Madoc ab Owain Gwynedd set sail in the *Gwennan Gorn* in 1170 to discover new lands. What is he said to have discovered?**

    a) America

    b) Greenland

    c) India

3. **Phil Campbell was born in Pontypridd in 1961. Which band did he join as lead guitarist in 1984?**

    a) The Rolling Stones

    b) Mötorhead

    c) Genesis

4. **Whose first book of poetry, published in 1949, was called *After Every Green Thing*?**

    a) Dannie Abse

    b) Alexander Cordell

    c) W H Davies

5. **In football, which club did Graham Williams captain to a 1-0 victory over Everton in the 1968 FA Cup Final?**

   a) Arsenal

   b) Chelsea

   c) West Bromwich Albion

6. **Who played the role of Warren Jones in the cult 1990s BBC drama *This Life*?**

   a) Jason Hughes

   b) Paul Rhys

   c) Rhys Miles Thomas

7. **In 1968, which band was the first act to be signed to the Beatles-owned Apple Records label?**

   a) Man

   b) The Iveys

   c) The Bystanders

8. **In rugby union, who was head coach of the Wales national side when they won a 2005 Six Nations Grand Slam?**

9. **Who in the early parts of the twelfth century wrote the Latin books *Prophetiae Merlini* and *Vita Merlini* about the wizard Merlin and *Historia Regum Britanniae* about the lives of the Kings of the Britons?**

10. **Which artist was born in Llangefni in May 1918, going on to be elected to the Royal Academy in 1974 and being knighted in 1999?**

Round 46

1. **Which of the following towns is situated in west Wales?**
    - a) Fishguard
    - b) Llangollen
    - c) Ebbw Vale

2. **Who played the role of Livia in the 1976 series *I, Claudius*?**
    - a) Rachel Roberts
    - b) Siân Phillips
    - c) Nerys Hughes

3. **Which National Eisteddfod Chair-winning poet's life is depicted in the 1994 Academy Award-nominated Welsh-language film *Hedd Wyn*?**
    - a) Cledlyn Davies
    - b) Dewi Morgan
    - c) Ellis Evans

4. **In which town would you find Agincourt Square, named after the famous battle where Henry V defeated French forces against significant odds, aided by Welsh archers?**
    - a) Brecon
    - b) Monmouth
    - c) Lampeter

5. In which year did Cwmbran's Rachel Rice win the reality television programme *Big Brother*?

    a) 2002
    b) 2008
    c) 2015

6. Where in Cardiff was a lighthouse erected in 1915 to commemorate the city's link with Captain Robert Falcon Scott's expedition to the South Pole three years previously?

    a) Cardiff Bay
    b) Cefn Mably Lake
    c) Roath Park Lake

7. Which club side became the 10th different winner of the Welsh Rugby Union Challenge Cup with a 32-19 victory over Pontypridd in 2012?

    a) Aberavon
    b) Glamorgan Wanderers
    c) Cross Keys

8. The song 'Barry Islands in The Stream' was a UK number one single in 2009 for Ruth Jones and Rob Brydon, playing their *Gavin & Stacey* characters Vanessa Jenkins and Bryn West. Which legendary Welsh singer appeared as himself on the song?

9. John Humphrys became the host of which BBC quiz programme in 2003?

10. Dafydd Wigley was a Plaid Cymru Member of Parliament from 1974 until 2001. Which constituency did he represent?

Round 47

1. **Which of the following actors has <u>not</u> appeared in a James Bond film?**
   a) John Rhys-Davies
   b) Jonathan Pryce
   c) Stanley Baker

2. **Which title did Helen Morgan attain in 1974?**
   a) Wimbledon singles tennis champion
   b) Miss World
   c) Princess of Monaco

3. **Where did St Deiniol establish the first cathedral in Wales in the sixth century?**
   a) Bangor
   b) Swansea
   c) Brecon

4. **How many prose tales together form the *Mabinogion*?**
   a) six
   b) eight
   c) eleven

5. **The Principality Permanent Investment Building Society was established in 1860. What was the business' income for the first year of trading?**
   a) £32
   b) £367
   c) £23,645

6. In which year did Brian Josephson win the Nobel Prize in Physics 'for his theoretical predictions of the properties of a supercurrent through a tunnel barrier'?

   a) 1954
   b) 1962
   c) 1973

7. Who was the three-times Olympic eventing gold medallist who was also World Champion in 1970 and 1982?

   a) Harry Llewellyn
   b) David Broome
   c) Richard Meade

8. Which Newbridge-born singer co-founded the Blitz club in London at the end of the 1970s, famously turning people such as Mick Jagger away at the door for not being suitably attired and spawning the New Romantic cultural movement?

9. Which Cardiff-born author has created a back catalogue of books that includes *A Column of Fire*, *World Without End* and *The Pillars of the Earth*?

10. *The Inn of the Sixth Happiness* was the second most popular film in British cinemas during 1958. North Wales formed a backdrop in the film to the true story of Gladys Aylward, a British maid who became a missionary in China. Who played this lead character?

Round 48

1. **Which was the only area in Wales to show a population decline between 2001 and 2011?**
   - a) Blaenau Gwent
   - b) Ceredigion
   - c) Denbighshire

2. **Which international retail chain did Llanelli-born Douglas Perkins establish with his wife Mary in 1984?**
   - a) Superdrug
   - b) Specsavers
   - c) Boots

3. **In which 1988-released Roald Dahl children's book did readers meet the characters Miss Honey, Miss Trunchbull and Bruce Bogtrotter?**
   - a) *Fantastic Mr Fox*
   - b) *Matilda*
   - c) *The Twits*

4. **If you were to purchase *cwrw* in a shop, what would you be buying?**
   - a) pasta
   - b) milk
   - c) beer

5. **What did Carmarthen ironmaster Philip Vaughan invent and subsequently gain a patent for in 1794?**
   - a) swivel chair
   - b) ball bearing
   - c) steam engine

6. **A 20-metre-high sculpture of a miner called the Guardian was unveiled in 2010. Which mining disaster is this in memory of?**

    a) Six Bells

    b) Senghenydd

    c) Abercarn

7. **Which character did Gareth Thomas portray in the BBC sci-fi series *Blake's 7*?**

    a) Vila Restal

    b) Kerr Avon

    c) Roj Blake

8. **In 2000, which Super Furry Animals album became the first Welsh-language record to reach the top 20 of the UK charts?**

9. **In rugby union, which former four-times capped Aberavon outside half held the role of Wales coach from 1982 until 1985?**

10. **Which 1938 film sees a newly qualified doctor played by Robert Donat accept a position in a south Wales mining village, where he's appalled by the conditions and political issues that he faces?**

Round 49

1. **In which year was Cardiff granted city status?**
   a) 1873
   b) 1896
   c) 1905

2. **Which lake is home to the rare freshwater fish called gwyniad?**
   a) Cosmeston Lake
   b) Lake Vyrnwy
   c) Bala Lake

3. **Gerald of Wales completed his 600-mile trek around Wales in April 1188. This journey led him to write one of the earliest travel books, called *Descriptio Cambriae*. Where was he born, circa 1146?**
   a) Manorbier Castle
   b) Chirk Castle
   c) Picton Castle

4. **Which type of food did Joe Cascarini become famous for producing and selling after establishing his Swansea business in 1922?**
   a) ice cream
   b) pies
   c) bread

5. **Which town has a style of knitted cap, reaching the peak of its popularity during the fifteenth and sixteenth centuries, named after it?**

   a) Monmouth
   b) Machynlleth
   c) Montgomery

6. **In which year was the S A Brain & Co. Ltd brewing company established on St Mary's Street, Cardiff by Samuel Arthur Brain and his uncle Joseph Benjamin Brain?**

   a) 1798
   b) 1882
   c) 1956

7. **Who played the role of Sheriff of Nottingham in the BBC series *Robin Hood*, which originally aired from 2006 until 2009?**

   a) Robert Pugh
   b) Keith Allen
   c) Dafydd Hywel

8. **Which book was published in Welsh in 1588, following ten years of translating by William Morgan?**

9. **What's the wall of water caused by the tidal surge of the sea being funnelled up the Severn Estuary and River known as?**

10. **Which band's back catalogue of songs includes 'Feeling A Moment', 'Just A Day' and 'Buck Rogers'?**

Round 50

1. **Julia Gillard became Australia's first female Prime Minister in June 2010. Where was she born?**
   - a) Llandudno
   - b) Barry
   - c) Porthcawl

2. **Which member of the surreal comedy group Monty Python was born in Colwyn Bay?**
   - a) Terry Jones
   - b) Eric Idle
   - c) John Cleese

3. **In which year was the Snowdon Mountain Railway opened to the public, carrying passengers from Llanberis to the peak of Wales' highest mountain?**
   - a) 1896
   - b) 1937
   - c) 1961

4. **In football, which of the following clubs did Billy Meredith, Mark Hughes and Clayton Blackmore all play for?**
   - a) Barcelona
   - b) Bayern Munich
   - c) Manchester United

5. **Marie N from Latvia won the 2002 Eurovision Song Contest with the song 'I Wanna'. Who came joint third for the UK with the song 'Come Back'?**

    a) Jessica Garlick

    b) James Fox

    c) Andy Scott-Lee

6. **In which sitcom that originally ran from 1968 until 1972 did Dowlais-born Richard Davies play the character Mr Price?**

    a) *Are You Being Served?*

    b) *Please Sir!*

    c) *Man About the House*

7. **Swallow Falls near Betws-y-Coed is a multiple waterfall system. Which river flows through this major tourist attraction?**

    a) Conwy

    b) Crafnant

    c) Llugwy

8. **Which Swansea-born newsreader was poached by the BBC in 1986 for a record salary of £100,000 per annum after 16 years with ITV?**

9. **Which brand of soft drinks, produced from a factory in Porth from the 1920s, was created by Rhondda grocers William Evans and William Thomas?**

10. **Which double act had a light entertainment sketch show which ran on BBC 1 for three years in the early 1970s?**

Answers

Round 1

1. a
2. c
3. b
4. c
5. c
6. b
7. c
8. Craig Thomas
9. Flat Holm
10. Dic Penderyn

Round 2

1. b
2. c
3. c
4. b
5. a
6. b
7. a
8. Ernest Willows
9. *Barbarella*
10. Thomas Telford

Round 3

1. a
2. b
3. b

4. a
5. c
6. c
7. a
8. (Penychain near) Pwllheli
9. Conservative
10. mail order

Round 4

1. a
2. c
3. a
4. b
5. a
6. c
7. b
8. Clough Williams-Ellis
9. Geoffrey Howe
10. pig

Round 5

1. c
2. a
3. c
4. b
5. b
6. c
7. c
8. Caerphilly
9. *Sea Empress*
10. Twm Siôn Cati

Round 6

1. c
2. b
3. a
4. b
5. b
6. b
7. a
8. Roy Jenkins
9. David Brunt
10. *The Cambrian*

Round 7

1. c
2. a
3. b
4. c
5. b
6. a
7. b
8. Abertillery
9. (pi)
10. Steve Jones

Round 8

1. a
2. c
3. b
4. c
5. c
6. b
7. a

8. raspberry
9. Tiger Bay
10. Jonathan Davies

Round 9

1. b
2. c
3. a
4. c
5. c
6. b
7. a
8. The Flying Pickets
9. Laura Ashley
10. *Lord of the Rings*

Round 10

1. c
2. b
3. a
4. c
5. b
6. a
7. b
8. Ramsay Bolton
9. Bryn Terfel
10. coxless four

Round 11

1. b
2. a
3. c

4. c
5. b
6. a
7. c
8. taekwondo
9. *Six O'Clock News*
10. Home Secretary

Round 12

1. c
2. b
3. a
4. c
5. a
6. c
7. b
8. Wales Empire Pool
9. Lawrence of Arabia
10. Pendine Sands

Round 13

1. b
2. c
3. c
4. b
5. a
6. a
7. c
8. (*Episode VI*) *Return of the Jedi*
9. Geraint Thomas
10. 'This Ole House', 'Green Door', 'Oh Julie' and 'Merry Christmas Everyone'

Round 14

1. b
2. b
3. c
4. c
5. a
6. c
7. c
8. *RMS Titanic*
9. Matthew Rhys
10. Marments

Round 15

1. c
2. b
3. a
4. a
5. c
6. b
7. a
8. Offa's Dyke
9. National Botanic Garden of Wales
10. Mathematics

Round 16

1. a
2. c
3. b
4. b
5. c
6. a
7. c

8. Gwrych Castle
9. Harry Secombe
10. Chapter Arts Centre

Round 17

1. c
2. b
3. a
4. c
5. b
6. c
7. b
8. Ray Reardon
9. Henry V
10. Penry Williams

Round 18

1. c
2. a
3. c
4. b
5. c
6. a
7. b
8. *Today*
9. 'It's Not Unusual'
10. Neil Kinnock

Round 19

1. c
2. c
3. a

4. b
5. a
6. b
7. c
8. Bonnie Tyler
9. Jonathan Pryce
10. Charles Stewart Rolls

Round 20

1. a
2. b
3. b
4. c
5. c
6. b
7. a
8. Newcastle Emlyn
9. Robbie Savage
10. *How Green Was My Valley*

Round 21

1. a
2. c
3. a
4. c
5. b
6. b
7. c
8. featherweight
9. *EastEnders*
10. Rowan Williams

Round 22

1. a
2. b
3. c
4. b
5. a
6. a
7. a
8. Gower Peninsula
9. Llandovery
10. Gareth Jones

Round 23

1. b
2. c
3. b
4. a
5. c
6. b
7. a
8. Sophia Gardens, Cardiff
9. Caernarfon Castle
10. Bertrand Russell

Round 24

1. b
2. c
3. a
4. a
5. c
6. c
7. b

8. Dan-yr-Ogof Caves
9. Pontypool
10. Rachel Roberts

Round 25

1. b
2. c
3. a
4. c
5. a
6. b
7. c
8. *The Prisoner*
9. Dave Edmunds
10. Winifred Banks

Round 26

1. c
2. a
3. a
4. c
5. c
6. b
7. b
8. James Callaghan
9. Ivor Allchurch
10. *Urdd Gobaith Cymru*

Round 27

1. a
2. c
3. c

4. b
5. c
6. a
7. b
8. Badfinger
9. Glyn Houston
10. Jim Driscoll

Round 28

1. a
2. b
3. b
4. a
5. c
6. c
7. a
8. *The Tube*
9. Jeremy Bowen
10. Ryan Giggs

Round 29

1. c
2. a
3. c
4. b
5. a
6. a
7. b
8. *The Clothes Show*
9. John Toshack and Joey Jones
10. Dwyryd

Round 30

1. a
2. a
3. c
4. c
5. a
6. c
7. b
8. Gilbern
9. Pete Fowler
10. Admiral

Round 31

1. b
2. c
3. c
4. a
5. b (*Black Book of Carmarthen*)
6. a
7. b
8. *Goldfinger, Diamonds Are Forever, Moonraker*
9. Speaker of the House of Commons
10. *Torchwood*

Round 32

1. a
2. b
3. c
4. b
5. c
6. a
7. c

8. Sully Island
9. Europol
10. John Oram

Round 33

1. a
2. a
3. c
4. a
5. b
6. c
7. b
8. Rhodri Morgan
9. Jon Pertwee
10. prop

Round 34

1. b
2. c
3. a
4. c
5. b
6. c
7. c
8. Declaration of Independence
9. 'Hit Me with Your Rhythm Stick'
10. Cardiff

Round 35

1. b
2. a
3. c

4. a
5. c
6. c
7. b
8. the Falklands War
9. Craig Thomas
10. Michael Laudrup

Round 36

1. b
2. b
3. a
4. c
5. a
6. c
7. b
8. Ivor Novello
9. The Spencer Davis Group
10. Michael Sheen

Round 37

1. a
2. b
3. c
4. c
5. c
6. a
7. b
8. Charlotte Church
9. Aneurin Bevan
10. 7(6 for Best Actor, 1 for Best Supporting Actor)

Round 38

1. c
2. c
3. b
4. a
5. b
6. a
7. b
8. Howard Marks
9. Carmarthen
10. Victoria Park

Round 39

1. b
2. a
3. c
4. c
5. a
6. b
7. a
8. Hear'Say
9. Dafydd Elis-Thomas
10. *Chicago*

Round 40

1. b
2. a
3. c
4. b
5. a

6. b
7. c
8. Dick Francis
9. Paul Whitehouse
10. 'Mercy'

Round 41

1. c
2. c
3. a
4. c
5. b
6. a
7. b
8. Ioan Gruffudd
9. Megan Lloyd George
10. Gower Peninsula

Round 42

1. c
2. b
3. a
4. a
5. b
6. c
7. a
8. Anthony Hopkins
9. Gary Sprake
10. Groggs

Round 43

1. a
2. b
3. c
4. a
5. c
6. a
7. c
8. Pontypandy
9. Felinfoel
10. Charles Stewart Rolls

Round 44

1. c
2. b
3. a
4. c
5. c
6. a
7. b
8. J P R Williams
9. Australia
10. Sean Mathias

Round 45

1. c
2. a
3. b
4. a
5. c
6. a
7. b

8. Mike Ruddock
9. Geoffrey of Monmouth
10. Kyffin Williams

Round 46

1. a
2. b
3. c
4. b
5. b
6. c
7. c
8. Tom Jones
9. *Mastermind*
10. Caernarfon

Round 47

1. c
2. b
3. a
4. c
5. b
6. c
7. c
8. Steve Strange (born Steven Harrington)
9. Ken Follett
10. Ingrid Bergman

Round 48

1. a
2. b
3. b

4. c
5. b
6. a
7. c
8. *Mwng*
9. John Bevan
10. *The Citadel*

Round 49

1. c
2. c
3. a
4. a
5. a (Monmouth Cap)
6. b
7. b
8. The Bible
9. Severn Bore
10. Feeder

Round 50

1. b
2. a
3. a
4. c
5. a
6. b
7. c
8. Martyn Lewis
9. Corona
10. Ryan Davies and Ronnie Williams

By the same author:

THE RUGBY UNION QUIZ BOOK

TEST YOUR KNOWLEDGE ON WORLD RUGBY

MATTHEW JONES

y Lolfa

£3.99

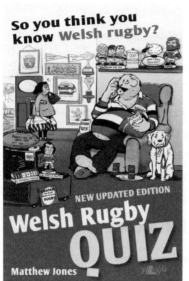

£3.95

£3.95

The Wales Quiz Book is just one of a whole range of publications from Y Lolfa. For a full list of books currently in print, send now for your free copy of our new full-colour catalogue. Or simply surf into our website

www.ylolfa.com

for secure on-line ordering.

TALYBONT CEREDIGION CYMRU SY24 5HE
e-mail ylolfa@ylolfa.com
website www.ylolfa.com
phone (01970) 832 304
fax 832 782